ANOTHER
SHORT &
SWEET
BOOK BY

Becky Brown

www.ShortandSweetBooks.com

THE
SECRET TO
ONLINE
SUCCESS

At
Axia College and
The University of Phoenix

Rebecca Brown, M.A.

Contents

INTRODUCTION

Dear student, congratulations on taking the time to pick up another book in addition to all those books you're required to read for class. I know it seems like you've already got enough work to do, but I promise you, this Short & Sweet Book is going to reduce your workload, not add to it!

First, let me tell you a little secret that took me

years to discover: the students who get the As in class are not always the smartest students, nor the ones that work the hardest, nor the ones that are most popular.

For the most part, the A students are the ones who have learned how to work smart—not hard!

The truth is, being the hardest working stiff isn't what gets you ahead in life. Those people out front winning the race, getting the promotions, earning the incomes, and making the grades are the ones who figured out how the system works. Then they made that system work for them.

In this book, I'm going to teach you the system work of online schools (and most on-ground schools), and how to budget your time so that you're spending it on those things that will help you earn As and get that degree.

How to Use This Book

I hope you can find the time to read this book from cover to cover. There is a lot of important information condensed into these few pages, and the better you know it, the more easily you'll be able to use it to consistently earn the A in your class.

You can also use this book as a reference. As you're taking a class, feel free to check the book for possible solutions to problems, answers to questions, and tips for speeding your studying and writing. The table of contents is a great place to learn what is here, and then you can focus your search on exactly the information you need, exactly when you need it.

Welcome to online school. I wish you the very best in your education. As always, I welcome your questions, comments, and concerns. You can reach me at:

BeckyBrown@ShortandSweetBooks.com.

1

HOW ONLINE SCHOOL WORKS (IN GENERAL)

Distance education, also known as on-line university, is a method of delivering college-level programs and courses to students who cannot sit in the same physical classroom as their instructors. The University of Phoenix and Axia College deliver the same rigorous academic education as on-ground universities, but allow you to participate and complete your class work by logging in to class from your home, your office, the library, or at the pool side, or even while on vacation. Now, you can complete your college degree from anyplace in the world, and on your schedule!

How You "Go to Class" Online

Online schools use software to deliver their courses, which you access with your computer and an Internet connection. You will be participating in online discussions with professors and classmates while completing course work such as reading, online tests, and paper writing.

Although some Internet schools require you to be online at a specific time each week, UOP and Axia college do not. You will be required to log in and participate in the class work a certain number of times each week, but choose those times based on your convenience. So, you can log in when the kids are napping, first thing in the morning, or in the middle of the night, if that's what you want!

Accelerated Classes

Online classes are generally accelerated classes. That means they encompass the same amount of reading, lectures, discussions, and assignments of a traditional class but you do it all in one-third of the time. A regular, semester-length, on-ground course lasts approximately fifteen weeks. The online course can last anywhere from five to ten weeks depending on the school.

At the University of Phoenix and Axia College, these classes last five weeks for upper-division courses, and nine weeks for the associate's degree courses, where each class is equivalent to a traditional 15-week course with all your class work compressed into just nine short weeks.

Additionally, at UOP and Axia College, you can attend class year round so that you can complete your course of study faster and earn your degree in much less time than it would take at a traditional university.

Course Load

The online student usually only takes one or two classes at a time (traditional students take three to five at a time) due to the heavy workload per class. But because UOP and Axia College offer courses that start every week, you can schedule your classes throughout holidays and summer vacation to complete your degree faster. Something you can't do in the more traditional schools.

You will also receive much more feedback on your assignments, as professors are required to evaluate your projects and papers substantively and frequently. The work you do turn in will be read, commented on, and returned to you within a week— and quite a bit sooner in most classes.

If you are a motivated student, you can be improving your study and writing skills each week, and incorporating those improvements into each new assignment. Very quickly, you'll have mastered the technique of learning using this new medium and will accelerate far beyond your on-ground brothers and sisters.

Asynchronous vs. Synchronous

Asynchronous courses never require that you be online at the same time as anyone else in your class, including your professor. The beauty of asynchronous courses is that you really can do that work any time during the day that you can fit it in, even if that is in the middle of the night.

At UOP and Axia College all classes are asynchronous.

Synchronous courses require students to meet online at a scheduled time each week. During these set times, faculty and students meet in a chat room where they can "talk" in real time. Although some online schools utilize the synchronous method, UOP and Axia College prefer to make their courses as flexible for students as possible.

Online Imitates On-Ground

UOP and Axia College try to make the online classroom as similar to the on-ground classroom as they can. So, just like a traditional college class, you will have reading assignments that relate to the projects that are due that week. Quizzes and tests will require you to know this material, and assignments are based on your learning from that week. They will be evaluated and graded each week.

IMPORTANT NOTE: Schools can rarely tell if you've just popped onto the class and looked. You have to **post something** to register attendance with the school's computer.

Additionally, classroom participation—which in this world means writing comments and answers to discussion questions each week—is highly regarded as one of the key learning tools. So you will find substantive participation is also required by both Axia College and UOP.

Participation vs. Attendance

<u>Participation</u> is measured by how many messages you actually post in your classroom discussing the course content with your classmates and professor.

In order for messages to be considered substantive, they must be about the subject of discussion that week, they must include specific references to the readings and comments on messages your classmates have written, and they must introduce a new idea or two.

Whether or not a message is substantive is a subjective evaluation that your professor makes when he grades your work each week.

<u>Attendance</u> is what the UOP or Axia College computer does automatically. It merely counts the number of posts you send to your class newsgroup each week. If you don't meet the attendance requirements (two posts each week), the computer notifies your academic advisor, who will contact you to make sure you're still on track in the course and will able to complete your studies.

This Is Nothing Like a Correspondence Course

Don't expect online classes, asynchronous or synchronous, to be anything like a correspondence course, where you can do the reading and polish off a few assignments in a couple of hours at the end of the term. You also cannot work ahead of your classmates to get everything completed in one or two weeks.

Every online class requires that you work along with your classmates— usually completing several assignments and projects by the dead-

---

The Difference between Attendance and Participation

Think of attendance as what your teacher does each day at the beginning of the class: she runs through her role sheet calling out names and checking off who is there that day. That's what the UOP and Axia College computer does every day in your online class.

Participation is how much you talk in class. If you sit in the back of the class and never raise your hand or participate in the class discussion, then you don't get participation points.

In online school, you "talk" by posting messages to your course. The more messages you post, and the more intelligent your comments, the more participation points you will earn.

line each week. Some faculty might allow you to work a bit in advance of the class, say, complete the reading or write a paper that isn't due until next week. But most will not.

Remember, this is a collaborative process just like any college class; you, your class-mates, and your professor are all working on the materials and concepts together. You all help each other learn and practice these new skills—which is a much more ef-fective and richer learning environment than trying to learn everything by yourself.

Vacations & Time Off

Because UOP and Axia College provide stu-dents with so much flexibility in how and when they attend class, there are fewer official school holidays. At this writing, there is at least one week off at Christmas and several days off at Thanksgiving. But the rest of the yearly holidays are optional days off for students. You decide whether or not to participate on any particular holiday. You will still be required to meet all assignment and participation deadlines for that week.

So if you really must have Valentine's Day off or risk losing what little personal life you have left, feel free to take it—just as long as you turn in your assignments and meet other participation requirements for the week.

Instructors Have Even Less Time Off

Remember, your instructor also gets the same limited vacation time each year, and she's been doing this for far longer than just the two years it takes to earn a degree. So, if during the week of Thanksgiving, you feel your instructor is a bit slow grading papers or isn't participating as much as usual, cut her a little slack, okay? She might return the favor one day.

2

MASTERING THE
TECHNOLOGY

You can't take classes on the Internet if you don't know how to use a computer and online software. Really, you just can't! So, if this is your first exposure to using the Internet, emailing, posting to newsgroups, and using Microsoft Word, you will simply have to invest the time (and, sometimes, money) into learning these new skills.

This may seem like self-apparent wisdom, but you would be surprised how many students (and even some faculty) I have met who don't factor this learning into their overall college plans, and as a result, spend many a night before a deadline tearing out hair because they can't make an assignment attach to their post.

In this chapter, I give you a basic tutorial about each of the processes that are absolutely necessary for taking online classes. But this is not a complete tutorial, since each piece of software can be very complex and requires entire books of its own to explain.

This will get you through the first class, but I strongly encourage you to use Appendix C in the back of this book to find online tutorials and texts that will give you a complete understanding of how this technology works. It is worth your time (and will save your hair) if you do.

Text-Based Education

At the time of this writing, almost all online classes are text based. That means you communicate with your professor and your classmates by writing messages that are posted to public message boards where everyone in your class (and anyone who has access to your class) can read them. This is because most students do not have the high bandwidth required to download and access very large files like video and sound. This is certainly the future of online classes, but it is not the present.

Online School Is Writing and Reading

So your work will entail typing on the keyboard of your computer and uploading what you've written to your classroom. You will also be heavily involved in reading: both what your professor has assigned you in textbooks and online eBooks, and what your professor and classmates have written.

If reading and writing are not your cup of tea, you might want to reconsider this kind of advanced education. Even with transcription software and voice recognition, there is simply no way to get around it; how you write will heavily affect your grades in any online class.

Attending Class

Classes are conducted on newsgroups (**NGs**). Newsgroups work very much like a real-world bulletin board. People "post" notes on the bulletin board and other people read those notes and post replies. [See an explanation of how to **post,** later in this chapter.]

The Class Website

Your classes will be available to you on the University of Phoenix website. Just log in to your home page and click the "Go to Class" icon. This will take you to a page that lists all the newsgroups for that class. You will see:

Main. The main classroom newsgroup for this class. This is where you will find notes from your professor, tips about that week's topics, discussion questions to answer, and posts from your classmates as they discuss the course work for that week.

Chat-Room. The place where you can chat about any topic with your class-mates and not interfere with the dis-cussions in the main newsgroup. This is also where you post your biogra-phy on the

IMPORTANT: Remember, in public NGs, everything you write can be read by your classmates and your professor. This is not the place to ask questions about your grades, problems with your assignments (unless it's something you think the whole class might be wondering about), or any other topics that you don't want to share with the entire class.

first day of class, and meet your fel-low classmates and instructor.

Please note, most professors do not spend much time reading in the Chat-room NG af-ter the first week, and do not count any of the posts in there when grading your class partici-pation. So, if you want credit for your wonder-ful, intelligent comments on class materials, you need to post them in the Main NG.

<u>Course-Materials</u>. The NG where you will find additional course materials posted by your instructor, including her contact information.

<u>Your Personal ING</u>. At Axia College (UOP does not use the personal NG), this is where you post your assignments and where your professor posts your grades. Only you and your professor have access to this NG.

<u>My Drafts</u>. If you ever start a post and feel you need to come back to it later before you send it (a very good idea if you're tempted to say something not very nice to someone in class), you can save it in your My Drafts folder. Later, you can make changes to this message, post it, or delete it without problem.

<u>My Sent Items</u>. This is the place where everything you send to the course newsgroups is saved. It's a good idea to check this folder after you send an assignment, just to be sure that it actually went to the NG like it should have. If it isn't in the My Sent Items folder, it wasn't sent and you should try sending again.

Farther down the left-hand side of the
web page you will also find links to:

My Inbox. This is where you receive email from
your professor and the University. You should
check it every single day.

Preferences. Where you can change how
your name looks when you post a message,
and change the size of your font.

Help. A link that sends you to the searchable
help pages.

Tips/FAQ. A link that sends you to a database
of tips and FAQs that will answer most
questions you have about the university and
this website.

Posting

Posting is how you get messages that you write
on your computer up to the school's computer. When you put a message on a bulletin board or newsgroup, it's called "posting"

the message. Messages on bulletin boards or newsgroups are called "posts." (Imagine that.)

The newsgroup is really just the server that the school has dedicated to your class. It's a computer in that school someplace. When you "post" a message, you're essentially sending an email to that computer, which it then displays for everyone to read (everyone who has access to that newsgroup).

No Deleting Posts

That's why once you send a post, you cannot get it back or delete it. You don't have the necessary access to delete posts from the school computer, although you might be able to delete them from your own computer. This is sometimes a hard concept for students to grasp.

Most posting software, like eCollege, do not even have an option for deleting posts. So be very, very careful what you send to your class.

Writing Readable Posts

Since much of your grade depends on the quality of your posts, it's very important that you proofread and revise those messages before you send them.

Remember, nobody in your class will likely ever see your face, including your professor. They won't see that snazzy haircut you just got, or the beautiful clothes you usually wear. They won't see how polite you are at work, or what a lovely personality you have. They only see your posts!

Your posts are your face now. So think

I like to explain it this way:

Imagine you wrote a letter, made a copy, and sent the copy to your mother.

Later, you regret the letter you sent to your mother, and you burn your copy. Does your mother still have her copy of the letter?

Of course she does! Your mother still has that horrible letter you wrote to her, because you burned your copy, not hers.

That's the way posting works. You are only sending a copy to the school's computer, and when you look at the newsgroups, you are only reading a copy of your post.

So deleting a post from your computer doesn't delete it from the school's computer. Just because you can't see the post anymore doesn't mean that others can't see it.

> ## Before you hit the send button, review what you've written:
>
> Is it legible?
>
> Do you sound LIKE YOU'RE SHOUTING?
>
> Do you use capital letters at the beginning of sentences and periods at the end?
>
> or do u wrt in some knd of shrt-hand tht is herd t reed?
>
> Hou is yerr speling? Our u usinng spelcheek?
>
> If I saw you on the street, would I recognize you by your writing?
>
> Does your writing make you look sloppy and haphazard, like a homeless person, or professional and intelligent?

about what you want your face to look like.

Archives

Everything you write in class is archived and kept by the school. So, if you lose your temper at a classmate—or <gasp> your professor—and write something you later wish you hadn't, it lives on forever in the archives of that school, and can be easily accessed by simply searching on your name.

It's also important to remember that anyone that has access to your classroom, such as administrators, academic counselors, or your classmates' spouses and kids, can read what is posted there.

All NGs (even those that only you and your Prof have access to), are **public space** and as such you should always be sure that anything you write there you want the public to read! Don't commit anything to print that you might later regret.

Attaching Documents

When you turn in a paper or other docu-ment to your professor for grading, you will have to **attach** that paper to your post to send it. Attaching just means that when you send the post to the school's server, a copy of the paper goes along with it.

Most software programs allow you to attach a document by clicking on a button that says "Attach" or on a little paperclip icon. Once you click on that button, a window will open up allowing you to type in the name of the document or find it on your computer.

33

The Required Software

UOP and Axia College require that you use the Microsoft Office Suite for your assignments. The Suite includes Microsoft Word, PowerPoint, Excel, and some other programs. Yes, it is expensive, but it is the cost of going to school. So look at it as a required investment, like textbooks. (Don't get me started on whether you *really* have to buy the books – you do if you want an A in the class.)

Microsoft Word (MSWord)

You will be required to write your papers in Microsoft Word (MSWord). This is not the same thing as Notepad, WordPerfect, or MSWorks. An MSWord file ends in ".doc"; unless you send a file that ends that way, your professors will likely be unable to open your documents. If they can't open them, they can't grade them. It is not your professor's responsibility to figure out how to open your assignments; it is your responsibility to deliver a document in the required format.

Freeware MSWord Compatible

The good news is that there are online versions of MSWord that you can get for free. One of these is at:

http://www.aplusfreeware.com/catego-ries/business/FreeMSWordAlternatives.html

With this software, you can read MSWord documents and write documents that can be opened by MSWord applica-tions. So you don't have to buy MSWord if you are really short on cash (or time).

35 ■

Save Papers as .txt or .rtf

In fact, saving any file as "Rich Text" or ".txt" or ".rtf" will likely ensure that your prof can read the paper.

Using Track Changes to Read Comments

You also have to be able to read your instructor's comments when he sends the paper back to you. Most professors use the MSWord editing feature, "Track Changes," to write comments on your paper. If you don't have MSWord to look at those papers, then you won't see these comments and you won't be able to improve for the next assignment.

So the final word? If you simply can't afford Microsoft Word, you can make do with one of the free applications—as long as you save the file in a version your prof can open. But in the long run you will lose out on points and grades. Considering how much money you're spending on college, is it really worth the penny saved?

MSWord Tutorials

If you need help learning to use your MSWord program, there are a number of free, online tutorials for you to use. Here are a few I like:

http://www.bcschools.net/staff/WordHelp.htm
http://office.microsoft.com/en-us/training/CR061832731033.aspx
http://www.internet4classrooms.com/on-line_word.htm
http://www.learnthat.com/courses/computer/word/
http://netforbeginners.about.com/od/learnmsword/Learn_Microsoft_Word_97_2000_2002_2003.htm

PowerPoint

This is the program that business people use on a daily basis to create visual pre-sentations. If you haven't run across it yet in work, you will. So take advantage of this opportunity to practice using it.

Most classes use PowerPoint in some way. Since PowerPoint compresses files to a very small size, and they can be easily converted to online presentations and even websites, it's a perfect tool for creating visual instructions to deliver to people via the Internet. You will probably be given PowerPoint presentations to help you understand materials in your courses, or they might be used in seminars and live chat sessions.

You will also likely be asked to create PowerPoint presentations for some of your assignments. Obviously, this means you need the program! I am not aware of any other program or freeware that is equivalent to PowerPoint, so this time you will simply have to cough up the dough and buy it.

Because this is such a great tool, it is very easy to get started using, but can also expand to accomplish even the most difficult tasks. Therefore, I recommend you take a look at the Microsoft online tutorials to help you master this program. Microsoft Office Suite offers a whole series of courses to help you master the PowerPoint skills from the most basic to the most complex. They can be found at:

http://office.microsoft.com/en-us/train-ing/CR061832731033.aspx http://www.bcschools.net/staff/PowerPointHelp.htm

These are certainly worth your time and ef-fort. (If you want to get those As, that is.)

Excel

Excel is a spreadsheet software program that also comes with your Microsoft Office Suite. Excel helps you do all things involv-ing numbers and calculations. Since I am an English professor, I can't help you with Excel, except to say that it's awfully han-dy when I want to make grade sheets.

But for you more math-inclined students, you'll find Excel to be your best friend. Use it wisely—learn the program! Here are tu-torials that I hear are quite good:

http://www.usd.edu/trio/tut/excel/
http://www.fgcu.edu/sup-port/office2000/excel/
http://www.bcschools.net/staff/ExcelHelp.htm

THE SECRET TO ONLINE SUCCESS

Instant Messaging (IMing)

When you send a message to someone who is online at the same time as you, and they send a message right back, that is called **instant messaging (IMing).** You and your friend are using an IM program that allows you to send and respond to each other in real time.

It is live chatting, meaning you are chatting with another person (by typing messages) at the same time as they are chatting with you.

Many schools employ IMing for their faculty office hours. That way, you know at least once a week you can reach your professor live, in person, and ask questions or discuss projects. I find this to be an essential tool for my students and often wonder why more of them don't use it.

With a chat window open, a student can ask me how to do a particular project, and I can work with them one-on-one until they completely understand the materials. I can even send them images, visual tools to help them understand what I am teaching.

If you want to make the grades in online school, I highly recommend you download one of the free IM software packages and learn to use it. Then contact your professor every time you have a question or are puzzled by an assignment. She is there to help you, and frankly, most professors I know sit bored and forlorn during their office hours, staring at an IM screen to which no one ever sends messages.

Where to Get Free IM Software

You can get the IM software from a number of places, including from AOL, which is listed below. You'll need to download the free software and sign up for an IM name. You don't have to have the same kind of software as your professor to IM them. You just have to know their IM name. (Mine is ProfBecky. You can IM me too!)

http://www.aim.com/index.adp

Outlook Express Software (OE)

UOP and Axia College deliver your class via newsgroups using Outlook Express (OE) or their own website.

OE is software that ships with most Windows-based computers. In addition to using OE to collect your email, you can set up newsgroup accounts on it. If you don't want to use the UOP or Axia College website to access your classes, you can use OE instead. It will do everything the website does, and a few things the website does not.

COMMUNICATING WITH YOUR SCHOOL

Knowing whom to contact for each kind of situation you run into while going to college is very important. You can waste hours trying to get hold of your professor for help with a password, when all that was needed was a quick call to tech support. You can spend days emailing your faculty advisor about a grade in a class, when your professor is the person who can help.

In this chapter, you will learn how an online university is organized and whom you should contact for each kind of situation in which you're likely to find yourself.

Three Main Parts of an Online School

In general, online colleges are divided into administrators, faculty, and technology people.

Administration

The administrators handle all the class scheduling; they decide what classes you will have to take to earn the degree you want to earn. They evaluate your past college credentials and decide if you get to skip ahead or if you have to start from the beginning. They help you get your school loans, and take your money too!

Faculty

The faculty are the content experts who teach you the content of their classes. When you're just starting out, they teach you basics like writing, study habits, math, etc. As you progress, you get into more specific content areas that directly relate to the degree you're trying to earn, such as business, nursing, IT, etc.

Professors are the ones who know your industry, know the theories and concepts you must learn, and have the task of teaching that to you.

Internet Technology (IT)

The technical people run the website, newsgroups, and email. They build the course web pages, and assign you login names and passwords. They set you up in your newsgroups and help you with anything involving software or
hardware.

The IT people are the go-to persons for all your technical issues. Don't be afraid to call them immediately when you have a problem—you're paying their salary, and they are there to help you. In most cases, your professor cannot help you with technical issues and can't even give you extensions on deadlines if you have a technical problem. So, whenever you have a software problem, call the Helpdesk first!

Making Friends with Your Professor

Your professor is your friend! Yes, she evaluates your work and sometimes gives you grades you don't like, but her job in the long run is to help you understand the materials. So don't get mad if you are frustrated or confused. Instead, reach out with questions, attend seminars, IM her, and show that you are willing to work.

Professors don't think less of students that get bad grades if those students are working hard to improve. They only give up on students who have already given up on themselves. So the more you show your willingness to try, the more your professor will bend over backwards to help.

Your Professor Didn't Write this Stuff!

In traditional colleges, the faculty create their own classes, decide what you have to read, and make up assignments for you—that is, they are generally in complete control of their classes.

In online school, the faculty do not create the classes. Course developers (administration) decide what students will read. They write the tests, they make up the assignments, and they write the syllabus. The professor is restricted to teaching what the course developer tells him to teach.

That means, even if you, your entire class, **and** your prof hate a particular assignment, there is nothing that he can do about it. You still have to do it, and he still has to grade it.

What Your Professor Is Required to Do

Your online professor has a very rigorous schedule that he is required to follow in order to meet the evaluation standards of UOP and Axia College. There are strictly enforced deadlines regarding when faculty must grade as-

47

signments, how frequently they must post to the discussion threads, and how quickly they must respond to emails. All of this is UOP and Axia College's way of ensuring that you, the student, are getting plenty of good teaching and attention from your professors.

Here is what all online professors are required to do. If your prof isn't doing this, then you should (politely) follow up with him.

Make This a Good Experience for You and Your Professor

Making this a good experience for you and your professor will go a long way toward earning that grade you desire. Sure, you can argue with your professor, flame them in class, send angry emails to them about grades you received, and file any number of grievances with the university and your academic advisor. But I guarantee, that won't change your grade one little bit. And, it might make it worse.

At the end of the day, your professor has the job of evaluating your work. That is what she is required to do. She gets into trouble if she tells everyone what a great job they did without ever telling them what they did wrong.

And, let's face it, that's why you're in school, isn't it? To learn? This is how learning works.

Your Professor Is on Your Side

But really folks, the truth is, your professor is on your side.

What Professors Think

Most professors are thinking about their last class and how well their teaching methods worked with those students and what didn't work at all. They're thinking about how they can minimize the busy work and improve the learning with this new set of students.

What Students Think

Most students are thinking about how quickly they can get through this class while doing the least amount of work necessary to earn the best grade possible (I've been a student, too).

What Your Professor Is Required to Do

- Grade your assignments within 7 days of the due date.

- Answer emails within 24-48 hours of receiving them.

- Post weekly grades that show your accumulative grade point average (GPA) for that class.

- Post to the discussion threads. Your professor will be joining and guiding the conversation on those discussion threads.

- Write substantive evaluations of your assignments.

- Hold office hours. At Axia College, your professor will be online from 4pm to 8pm in your time zone, Sunday through Thursday.

- Follow all the rules the school has set regarding how to grade and evaluate each student. Things like how late they can accept papers, how they must count students' participation, and how many As they are allowed to give out, all come from the administration, and the faculty member has to follow those rules.

And hoping they have a professor that writes clearly and is willing to help out if they get lost.

You both want the same thing! That is, to make this the most productive learning experience with the least amount of pointless busy work.

Your Professor Is Your Partner

You and your professor are partners during your time in this class. Your professor wants to help you understand the materials, and you want to understand the materials. So it seems like there should never be any conflicts.

Make Life Easier for Both of You

If you want to make a good grade in a class, and do your professor and yourself a favor, make life easier for both of you. If you don't understand an evaluation, just ask your professor for clarification. He will be happy to give it to you.

If you didn't get a response to a post on the newsgroup, don't assume it is because your professor doesn't like you. He has a lot of messages to read and probably missed yours.

If you didn't get a response to an email—and it's been more than 24-48 hours—email again! Sometimes emails don't go through, or you had the wrong email address, or your professor meant to answer and got distracted and forgot. There is no reason for your professor to **refuse** to answer an email (unless it is inflammatory), so don't assume that's what happened.

Indeed, the best advice I can give you about your professor is to remember he is a human being, not a computer. He makes mistakes, gets sick, spaces out, forgets, and gets his feelings hurt just like you do. So always give your profs the benefit of the doubt; they will appreciate your consideration, and that will always be in the back of their minds somewhere when they are deciding if you deserve a B+ or an A- on that paper!

What to Do if You Think Your Professor Has Made a Mistake

Yes, even big brains with Ph.D.s make mistakes! If you think your professor has, just ask. Don't ask by ranting and raving, or sending long emails that explain why your professor is stupid and irresponsible for making that mistake. Just ask.

Don't assume that your professor is deliberately giving you a zero when you really did turn the assignment in on time; just ask.

Ask the way you would want to be asked if you were the professor, and you'll likely hear back "Oops! I goofed. Let me fix that right now for you."

Of course, sometimes the mistake is yours—which is another reason to ask politely, and not belligerently. It's terribly embarrassing when you try to shame someone for making a mistake, and they end up turning right around and shaming you!

How to Contact Your Professor

Your professor works remotely just like you do, either from home or from his professional of-

53

fice, and it isn't appropriate for him to give out the phone number of either of those places.

However, Axia College requires that their professors provide a phone number where students can reach their intructors, or leave a message. These teachers often use a special voice mail company that will take a message and contact them when a student calls.

Email

The best way to communicate with your professor is by using email or the newsgroups. Remember, your professor is also working asynchronously, just like you. So don't assume while you are online and struggling with an assignment that your professor is online too, waiting for your email.

In most cases, you'll have a lag time between when you email the prof and when you hear back. So that means—and this is **very important**—that you can't ask a question about an assignment an hour before the assignment is due! Your prof just won't be able to get back to you in time.

Even at Axia College, where faculty are required to be online from 4pm to 8pm, Sunday through Thursday, to answer your questions, you can't be sure that something won't happen to delay a reply (like your post not posting to the newsgroup immediately, or your professor simply missing your question, or the assignment falling due on a day that is not your professor's office hours).

Therefore, always give yourself at least 48 hours to work on your assignments before they are due so you have time to ask questions and get the answer, and make the changes!

Office Hours

At Axia College, your professor is required to keep office hours from 4-8pm during your time zone, Sunday through Thursday.

That means during those hours of those days, your professor is online, watching for your questions and waiting for you to contact him.

Navigating Administration

The school administration keeps track of things like your overall GPA, the classes that you've completed for your degree, the number of classes you still have to take, and everything that has to do with finances and school loans.

You know what? The administration is made up of humans too, and they also make mistakes! So if you are locked out of a class, didn't receive your textbook, didn't get your loan disbursement, think you already took this class, or any other questions that have to do with your enrollment in this school, ask! They will be happy to check it out for you, fix it if they've made a mistake, or explain it if they haven't.

Working with Your Academic Advisor

UOP and Axia College assign their students to an academic advisor. This is the person that you work with one-on-one to help you navigate the confusing and often frustrating job of earning your degree.

Your academic advisor makes sure that you're taking the classes you should be taking, that you're passing those classes, and that your loans are paying for those classes.

Your professors will contact your academic advisor if your GPA falls below a certain grade (usually, a D), and the academic advisor will contact you. They want you to complete your course of study, too, and they'll do anything they are allowed to do, to help you get that GPA backup.

Remember, although the Academic Advisor is your guide and advocate through the university system, she has to play by the rules, too. So don't ask her to do anything that is illegal or unethical.

Filing Grade Grievances

On those occasions when you do find yourself in a class where you feel that you're not getting a fair shake from your professor (rare, but they do sometimes happen), you can file what's called a "grade grievance" to protest the grade you were given.

All you do is fill out a form—your academic advisor has it—that includes your explanation for why you think that grade should be changed, and file it with the school. A panel will review this form and make a final decision. That panel usually includes the chair of the department (your professor's boss) and the dean of the school (your professor's boss's boss).

No One Will Re-Grade the Assignment

It's good to keep in mind, though, that professors are allowed great leeway in how they evaluate and grade assignments. After all, they are the content expert. They know better than anyone else in administration whether you've really learned the concepts in your class or not. No one will second-guess your professor's professional evaluation of the work you turned in.

That means that even if you file a grievance, you don't get a new grade from a new professor. Rather, the panel will look to see if there is any evidence of prejudicial treatment by your professor: if all your emails were replied to, if you were given adequate time to discuss this, and if your professor was **responsive** to your concerns (but not necessarily if they changed their mind or changed your grade). If everything looks about average for a usual class, then the grade remains the same.

Contact Your Professor Instead

Grade grievances rarely result in a changed grade. In my experience, you will have much more success getting a grade changed if, in a very friendly manner, you contact your professor and ask them to take another look at that assignment.

If you can point out that you did do the things your professor said you lacked, then he might reevaluate that grade and give you a better one.

Remember how professors sometimes make mistakes? Sometimes they also make mistakes reading papers and evaluating assignments.

Here are the things academic counselors are allowed to do:

- Help you figure out how your online class works; show you where to find your readings, the syllabus, etc.
- Help you understand your grade sheet and teach you how to read it.
- Give you study tips to improve your learning skills.
- Refer you to academic success programs that will help you with any areas in which you are struggling.
- Contact your professors to see if there is anything you can do to make up missing or less-than-passing work.

Here is what your academic counselor cannot do:

- Change your grade in any class or on any assignment.
- Force your teacher to change your grade.
- Evaluate assignments or grade them.
- Require your teacher to accept late work, extend deadlines, or offer extra credit.
- Let you into a class you've been locked out of for non-payment of tuition.
- Let you skip classes.

So, once again, I recommend that instead of jumping right to the dramatic act of filing a grievance with the school (something that always irritates professors, because they are forced to fill out a lot of extra paperwork and defend their actions), that you nicely ask your professor for a second look.

Getting to Know Your Peers

Your classmates can be of great assistance to you in successfully (and spectacularly) passing your classes. Remember, they are a whole bunch of people like you: adult learners with specific academic and career goals, trying to balance work, family, and school. They are probably your most sympathetic allies.

Making Friends

If you make friends, your classmates also bend over backwards to help you. In my classes, I am always amazed at the caring, affectionate, and helpful attitudes shown by students. They exchange IM names, tutor each other through the hard parts, proof-read and copy edit for each other, and hold virtual hands when someone has had a rough week, or pat each other on the back when they've had a small success.

So turn to your fellow students first and last. Don't be afraid to open up and make friends. You'll probably see them in class after class as you go through your courses.

How Your Classmates Can Help You

Classmates can help you understand the reading by discussing the ideas for that week. In fact, that's what the discussion questions are supposed to help you do. Remember, two brains are better than one, and 20 can give you whole new insight on the subject matter.

So instead of only relying on your professor to explain the material, try to work it out together, with everyone else in the class. You'll be amazed at all the new perspectives and might find that the ideas that surface during a class discussion will be just the ideas that earn you an A on the paper.

What Not to Say to Your Classmates (or to Your Professor)

That being said, here are a few words of caution: remember that your classmates all come from different parts of the country, different backgrounds, and different life experiences. Don't expect them to see the world exactly the way you do, and don't expect them to always agree with you.

If you find that you heartily disagree with something a classmate has posted, it's okay to politely say you disagree and explain why. It is not okay to flame them! (This goes for your professor, too.)

Free Speech in the Classroom

The classroom is meant to be a forum where people feel free to discuss many ideas and disagree with each other. I have seen entire classes go mute after one student flames another for an opinion with which she disagrees.

After all, nobody wants to voice his opinions if there is a risk of being verbally attacked.

Although we all know that saying,
  "Sticks and stones will break my bones,
  but words will never hurt me."

It just isn't true! Words *do* hurt. And they hurt a lot more if you can't hear the tone of voice with which they have been said. So . . .

Watch Out for That Tone!

The worst thing about this medium is that whatever you write stays right there for people to read over and over. So the emotions of a moment become a fixture in the classroom that is impossible to forget or ignore.

Please, please, don't write anything harsh or less than friendly in any message you send to your classmates or professor (or anyone, actually). If you feel your blood pressure rising, step away from the computer. Take a deep breath. Take a break of a couple of hours or even a day or two until you can see clearly again. Then if you must respond, re-spond with a very polite, very nice reply.

It's likely that the person that upset you is feeling bad about what she wrote, too, and wishes she could take it back. Be the bigger person, and make it nice for everyone again.

3

THE ALL-IMPORTANT FIRST DAY OF CLASS

It's the first day of class, and you didn't even get new school clothes! But that shouldn't dampen your enthusiasm to meet your professor and your classmates. This is not the day to play shy, or slack off and skip checking in, or just post one "checking in" post and promise yourself to read everything tomorrow.

The A student has already started reading, downloading and planning his course calendar. You should do that, too! So pull out your biography, revise it from the last time you used it, and post it on the meet-and-greet thread and get started with the class!

Make a Folder for Your Class

The first thing you should do whenever you start a new class is to make a folder on your computer where you keep all the materials for that class, and every assignment and paper you write in that class.

It's important to remember where you saved all your paper for each class, and what you named them! If you need to attach your paper to your post, you'll need to know where to find it. And if later, you need to find assignments that were graded and sent back to you, you'll have your own archive of your work on your hard drive.

If you have more than one class, make a

folder for each class.

Then when you save the paper, save it using your full name and the name of the assignment. Remember, your professor will be downloading a lot of papers to her computer each week to grade. If you just call your paper "Assignment.doc," how will she know whose paper that is once it's on her computer?

So use your name and the name of the assignment as the document name. That would look something like this:

BeckyBrown_PersuasivePaper.doc

This tells the professor who wrote the paper, and which assignment it is for. If your professor loses your paper, you will have to re-send it at best, and at worst, you might get a zero on it. So save everyone the confusion and name your assignments appropriately.

Introducing Yourself

The first thing you will do with any online class is introduce yourself. In some classes, you actually get graded on your introduction! For most, though, this is merely a way to jump-start the students, get them posting on the first day, and get them engaged with their classmates and professors right away.

Prepare Your Biography

You might want to take a few minutes to write a short (200-300 words) biography of yourself to post for your classmates and professors. This should not be your life story. Don't start with your birth and work your way through 45 years of life! Nobody will read that. Instead, think of a pleasant, clever way to talk about who you are and why you're in this class.

Remember, these people will never see your face or hear your voice, yet we are all human beings that need to have a picture of some kind in our minds when we communicate with others. So **write** a picture for your classmates.

LEAVE OUT THE PERSONAL INFORMATION

I want to warn you about writing very personal, revealing biographies. Remember, this is a professional school and these are all strangers. Although you may learn to know and even feel great affection for some of them, don't share those most intimate moments of your past with your classmates and teacher.

Don't talk about your heroine-addicted brother or your alcoholic mother, or the terrible divorce you're presently going through. Those are confessions for your diary, not for school.

The Internet is much too public a place to be exposing yourself this way. Just as you wouldn't stand up in a room full of strangers and tell them all about how you lost a child last year and have been in and out of alcohol treatment centers to cope with your relapse, you should not tell your online classmates such matters.

I know it's tempting to pour out your secrets and send them off into the stratosphere, but there are real people reading this bio. So keep it friendly but superficial.

The Syllabus

The first thing you'll need to do (after you post your biography) is to download, print, and **read** the syllabus.

Print the Syllabus!

I recommend printing it out, even though you can always access it on your computer. If it's in print, on your desk, you'll be much more likely to check it when you have a question or shen you start to wonder when that next project is due.

Above all else, you want to minimize the busy work—that means arranging everything so you are at your most efficient. So put that syllabus on your bulletin board, in the giant clip next to your computer, or at the front of the three-ring binder you've created for this course so you can get to it quickly.

Read the Syllabus!

Now take out your Post-Its and start reading the thing.

What? Read the syllabus? Am I mad?? Don't they all say the same thing?

Absolutely not! The syllabus is your contract with your professor. You must read it so you know what your professor expects of you, and what you can expect of your professor.

The syllabus tells you the textbooks that are required, the assignments that you'll be doing, the reading and the dead-lines, the late policy, grade rubrics, and a myriad other important information.

Sure, if you don't care about your grades, go ahead and rely on your prof to remind you when assignments are due. Sometimes that works. (Not in my classes, of course. I never remind anyone because all my stu-dents are adults. I know that adults take responsibility for their own work. They're spending big bucks on school and they make sure that their money is well spent by knowing exactly when everything is due.)

What to Do While You Read the Syllabus

Don't do your nails, watch the game, or fix dinner. As you read your syllabus, you'll want to be doing a couple of things: noting the class rules and writing your Assignment Schedule.

As you follow the steps below, I want you to have a pad of Post-Its next to you so that when I tell you to, you can write a note and post it in your syllabus.

Step 1: Understand the Class Rules

You want to understand the rules for each new class. Although UOP and Axia College have general rules that govern things like midterms and attendance, each professor can have his own rules about whether assignments can be turned in late (the Late Policy) and how many points are deducted for those late assignments, whether extra credit is offered, and whether assignments can be redone if you get a bad grade, and many other extremely important facts.

The A student learns all these rules and policies on the first day of class so that she

Reading Instructions

It might seem self-evident that you should read the instructions in order to understand the task or assignment. And yet, so many students never take the time to do that. In their eagerness to get on with the assignment, they skip the most important part!

The A student doesn't skip anything. He knows that if the professor has taken the time to write this down, it's worth reading. So the A student knows that the rough draft must be posted in APA format and sent as an attachment, whereas the C student didn't realize that and loses points because the paper is not formatted correctly.

Always read the instructions. No instruction is so minor it can be ignored.

doesn't make a rookie mistake like missing a deadline or counting on extra credit to pull up her grade when, as it turns out, that prof doesn't offer extra credit.

Know the Late Policy

Put a sticky note by the late policy in the syllabus. Then **read** the late policy so you can be sure you understand it.

Every instructor will have a late policy. It is either a policy dictated by the school, by which the instructor must abide, or a policy they create and enforce themselves. I recommend you do everything in your power not to turn in assignments late.

Aside from losing points for turning in late assignments, the other major disadvantage is that most classes are constructed so that each assignment builds on the last. If you skip one, or start getting behind, you'll find it impossible to understand or complete the next. It gets worse and worse each week.

Extensions on Assignments

Most professors have had enough dealings with students to know how tempting it can be to tell a really tall tale in hopes of getting an extension on an assignment or forbearance on late penalties.

Most students are amazed to find out that we hear these stories four or five times **a week.**

The Ever-Mounting Pile of Late Assignments

On the few occasions that I have offered forbearance on late assignments and allowed students to get very far behind in their class work, I've regretted it. Assignments are like bills; it only takes being behind on a couple for it to start weighing on even the most diligent of us—it just keeps mounting and mounting, until it is an un-scalable mountain of work.

The Student Who Gets an Extension Rarely Turns in That Assignment

Typically, the student who gets more than a week behind on class work can never catch up. I discovered the hard way that I am doing my students no favor by letting them turn their work in late. It's better to complete assignments as due. So find out on day one if your professor allows extensions, and what kind of rules she may have about using them.

77

Office Hours

Put a sticky note on the page by the office hours so you know when you can reach your prof.

Contact Information

Put a sticky note next to your prof's email address and IM name (write the email address on the sticky so you can read it without opening the syllabus!

First Day Tasks

Now that you've read and understood all the rules, it's time to get started on the organization for this course. You need to organize your time for the entire length of the course on the first day if you want to be sure you're on top of all the deadlines and don't make any rookie mistakes like missing a due date.

Start Your Assignment Calendar

The most important thing you need to do

Four Easy Steps for Writing Your Assignment Calendar

STEP 1. Write down the title of the assignment on the date it is due on your calendar.

STEP 2. Next to that, write how many pages the assignment is (or the word count).

STEP 3. Now estimate how long you think it might take you to do that assignment. You'll get better at guesstimating this as you take more classes and do more projects. So start by guessing high:

Persuasive Paper: 3500-3700 words
4 days research
2 days writing
1 day revising
Total = 7 days

STEP 4. Now that you know how much time you will likely need to complete the project, count backward from the due date and mark on your calendar when each of these deadlines should be met.

One day before the due date:
start revising the paper.

Three days before the due date:
start writing the paper.

Seven days before the due date: start researching the paper.

today, the first day of class, is to make your **Assignment Calendar**. (See inset box.)

The best way to do this is to print out an actual blank calendar that you can write on. Then, as you go through the syllabus week by week, you can write in the name of the assignment on the date it is due in your calendar.

That way you know if you are falling behind and need to work late and catch up, or have a little extra time and can take a break and go to the park with the kids!

Write a Paper Criteria List

It always surprises me when I get a paper from a student that has little or nothing to do with what was assigned. I used to ask myself: "Are they just turning in any old paper, and assuming I'm not reading them and so I won't know the difference?"

Then I discovered that my students weren't carefully reading the requirements for each assignment and so they weren't being careful to meet those requirements in their papers.

Imagine this: your boss asks you to send out letters to the board of directors, changing a meeting time from Tuesday to Thursday. You send out a couple of letters to some share holders to say the meeting has been changed from Monday to Friday. Do you think your boss will be happy? Likely not! You haven't done what she asked you to do—even though you did do **something**.

"Something" is not enough, for bosses or for teachers!

You Don't Get Credit for Trying

You won't even get credit for doing part of the job since you didn't accomplish the goal of this task—informing the Board of the new meeting time).

The same is true in school. Unfair as it may seem, you are graded for the product you create, not the effort you put into it. So if you find yourself laboring over an assignment, take a breather and see if there is a smarter, faster way to do it.

Your Professor Grades How Well You Achieved the Criteria

Each project is designed to help you practice the skills and concepts you've learned in the class that week. So each project has special requirements that you must follow. Your professor will be evaluating your work based on how well you met the requirements for that project.

To prevent any mistakes and ensure that you meet all requirements for your paper, you must write a **Criteria List** for each assignment.

Writing the Criteria List

At the beginning of each week, take a look at the project that is due that week. Make yourself a numbered list of the requirements that you will have to meet. (See inset box.)

Now that you have this handy list, you can start planning your paper. Keep checking the list to see that you're remembering to

Persuasive Paper Criteria List

1. Must be 2500–3500 words

2. Must be in APA format

3. Must use three to five sources

4. Only two sources can be from the Internet

5. Can't use Wikipedia at all!

6. Must be on an approved topic (have to get approval from prof by day two)

7. Must use the concepts we've been discussing in class

8. Must incorporate peer review comments in final draft

9. Due in the dropbox on Weds of next week!!

do everything. When you've finished your first draft of the paper, check it against this list again to make sure you've done everything you should. Pretend you're the professor—be hard on yourself! Make yourself rewrite anything that you've done wrong.

If you make a Criteria List and check it twice (or three times), you'll at least know that you won't lose any points for foolish mistakes like posting your paper to the thread instead of the dropbox, or not using APA style when you format it.

4

THE SMARTEST STUDENT DOES NOT GET THE A

The A student gets the best grades in the class not because she was worlds better than everyone else in class, but because she was a tiny bit better than anyone else.

Most students (the ones who get Bs and Cs) think that A students must be brilliant scholars, much smarter than the average

student. But the truth is, the difference between an A and a B is often very small. A
matter of degrees. A matter of detail.

The Devil (and the A) Is in the Details

The A student always reads the directions
carefully so that she is following them exactly. She proofreads so that her papers
are free of all typos and other errors, and
she makes sure her formatting is correct.

In other words, almost anyone can get
an A if they pay attention to the little details that the B and C students never do.
In this chapter, I'm going to tell you what
those details are so that you can give them
the attention that the A student does.

Read Your Professor's Comments

Read the comments the professor makes.
The feedback your professor gives you is ex-

actly what you have to do to the next time
(wasn't that nice of her to just tell you?);
so use them and understand them.

This isn't about punishment—this is how college works. You try something, the professor tells you what worked and what didn't,
and then you try something else. Eventually,
you'll be writing A assignments all the time.

Use Your Professor's Comments

So take those comments
from your prof and write
yourself a "punch list" so
you can be sure to make
those corrections on
your next assignment.

A Punch List is some-
thing contractors write
at the end of a long
project. It's a list of
mistakes that have to
be fixed before the
client will pay him.

Check Your Weekly Grade Report

The first thing you must always do is check
your grades. Check the grade you earn on
your assignments, check your weekly grade,

and check your GPA for the entire course as it changes with each new assignment.

You should also be checking your overall college GPA since some employers want to know what that is. But what I really want you to get into the habit of doing is knowing exactly where you stand from day to day.

Don't Be Surprised by Your Grades

The A student is never surprised—he knows how he's doing in every class, at any given moment, and so he knows if he needs to exert himself a little more to pull his grade up, or if he can afford to take a break and watch that game on TV.

Check the Grade on Each Assignment

Check the grade you receive on each assignment. Don't be afraid to look! Even if it is painful at first, you **must** know how you did in order to know how to improve.

Double-Check the Math

Then check that she's added up your points correctly and that if there is a grade,
it is the right one for that amount of points, or if it is a percentage, that the percentage was worked out correctly. Always do this for every assignment.

Even Professors Make Mistakes

Here's another secret: even college professors can be bad at math! I am quite terrible at math and rely heavily on a calculator to help me work out the grades for my students. Even so, and although I am very careful, I have still been known to make a mistake or two. And if my student didn't catch it, I probably wouldn't have to know it so as to change it.

So don't be a trusting fool! Check your professor's math—make sure the addition and subtracton are right. Make sure he's given you the grade you earned. Point out nicely if he's made a mistake. Profs don't mind changing grades if it's their mistake, so don't be afraid of that.

How to Calculate Your Grade Each Week

Even if your professor doesn't provide you with a letter grade each week, it's very easy for you to figure it out for yourself. First, you'll need to get out your syllabus and find the *percentage to grade conversion chart*. Every school provides this. It is a chart that tells you what letter grade you will get for a percentage you've earned in class. It's usually in your syllabus, but if it's not there, just ask your prof.

If your professor only gives you a point value for each assignment, there is a simple mathematical formula for figuring out what percentage you've earned so far. Take the total

---

Number of points you've earned so far
Divided by
Number of points it is possible to earn so far

---

number of points you have earned so far in the class, and divide it by the total number of points it is **possible** to earn so far.

CHECK YOUR GRADE

If I earned a total of 25 points total for weeks one and two, and it is possible to earn a total of 30 points for weeks one and two, then my grade so far, as a percentage, is 83%.

$$25/30 = .83 \text{ OR } 83\%$$

Then I look up my grade conversion chart to see that an 83% is a B:

100-95%	A	82-80%	B-	69-66%	D+
94-90%	A-	79-76%	C+	65-63%	D
89-86%	B+	75-73%	C	62-60%	D-
85-83%	B	72-70%	C	Below 60%	F

* Remember, each school uses their own grading scale, so you have to get the grade conversion chart from your school to find out your grade. This is just an example.

This gives you your score as a percentage. Then look up the percentage-to-grade conversion chart to see what grade that is.

Why Calculate Your Grade Each Week?

The A student knows what grade he's earning from week to week in any given class. He does not wait until the last week to wonder if he's earning an A. He already knows! That means he's so on top of watching his grade sheet that he also knows if he's slipping below that A each week.

Why is that important? Because if you see your weekly grade slip below an A, then you can start *immediately* to change what you're doing to get the grade back up.

Every grade you earn on every assignment averages into your final grade. And the more assignments you complete, the harder it will be to change your final grade.

It's Easy to Change Your Grade at the Beginning of the Course

In the first few weeks, if you miss an assignment or get a bad grade on an assignment, you can see your grade change from an A to an F very quickly! But you can change it back to an A pretty quickly too.

Not So Easy Near the End of the Course

But by the time you're into the last few weeks of classes, you've completed so many assignments that each assignment has less of an effect on your final grade. That means the grade you're presently earning becomes very hard to change.

That's why it's important to always know what grade you're earning and work imme- diately to improve it if you drop below your target grade. Don't tell yourself it's okay be- cause you have eight weeks to go. By the time you've reached the fifth week, you will find it very difficult to raise your grade at all.

Submitting Assignments

Each week you will be asked to complete and submit assignments based on the learning for that week. Aside from following directions and meeting the criteria for each individual assign- ment, there are some very basic guidelines you should follow when submitting an assignment.

First, assume that all assignment should be pasted into the body of your post and not submitted as an attachment unless the directions specifically tell you otherwise.

Attachments Carry Viruses

Attachments carry and transmit computer viruses, so they can be difficult to handle. Attachments that are transmitted through a dropbox (which you find in eCollege software and some others) are cleaned before being downloaded, so the viruses, if any, are wiped off them.

For this reason, it's always better to only submit attachments when your professor specifically calls for them.

Styles and Formatting Require Attaching

Any document that has to have MLA, APA, or other specific formatting **must** be an attachment since those formatting requirements can't be done on a post.

When you do attach a file, be sure that you have used a logical name to save it. That file name should include your first and last name, and the name of the assignment:

Becky_Brown_PersuasivePaper.doc.

That way, when your professor downloads your file, she doesn't end up with 15 documents called "mypaper.doc"!

Always Turn in Your Best Work (Even for Rough Drafts)

Also, remember that any assignment you submit for a grade must be the best product you can create to date. That means no typos, no spelling errors, no strange line breaks or extra pages, and no annotated notes left over from when you were proofreading it. It should be a clean, beautiful, perfect paper that you are proud to put your name on.

6

HOW TO STUDY SMART NOT HARD

I have a whole book devoted to study habits; they are just that important! The way you study has everything to do with what grade you'll earn in a class. I've learned this all by trial and error. I have spent late nights reading, underlining, taking notes, highlighting, burning the midnight oil, etc., all to earn a C in class. I have also read swiftly, taken

Smart Notes, and compiled Fast Sheets in one-third of the time—and gotten As every time!

For the full "Study Smart Not Hard" program, you'll want to check out my book *How to Study Smart Not Hard (and Still Get the A)*.[1]   However, here is a quick lesson you can use right now.

Smart Notes™

Don't spend hours and hours reading and re-reading material that makes no sense to you! That's not smart, it's just hard.

Instead, follow these simple directions for taking smart notes that will help you read, understand, and remember!

STEP 1: Chapter Overview

1. Start by reading the Table of Contents for the chapter you've been assigned to read.

The table of contents is a great place to get an overview of what each chapter and section is about. I always start with the table of contents in any book I have to read, so I know what's coming, and have some idea what to expect. I get my mind ready to absorb that material.

2. Write in the margin next to the chapter you're going to read, what it's about in your own words.

It's very important that you actually write this by hand, and that you do it in your own words. One way you learn is by rephrasing things. It forces you to think about something, rather than letting it go in your eyes and out your ears without ever sticking to your brain! So putting an idea into your own words helps you learn it. Here's an example of what that lit-tle note might look like:

"This chapter is about the First Amendment."

Easy, right?

3. Next, look to see if there are any subheadings for

that chapter.

If there are, write next to each subheading what that section is about. Here's what that might look like:

> "This section is about the Free Speech clause."

> "This section is about freedom of the press."

> "This section is about the establishment of religion."

WHY WRITE BY HAND?

The reason you actually write by hand is that doing something physical while trying to learn helps you learn! Physically writing those ideas down is speeding your learning.

Later, when you will type up these notes, that is another, a different kind of physical activity, and that too will add to the speed with which you learn and remember.

If you don't want to mark your book, write on stickies and stick them to the appropriate places in the book. That's still writing, after all. And if you are reading an eBook, print it off and write on those pages.

---

4. Now, turn to that chapter and read the first paragraph and write in the margins next to it the main idea of this chapter.

You should only have to read the introductory paragraph to know what the main idea is, although sometimes you have to read a couple of paragraphs—just don't read too much! Write your short synopsis right next to that first paragraph.

Suppose the first paragraph looked like this:

> "The First Amendment of the Constitution guarantees some rights that our founding fathers believed to be essential to a free and functioning democracy. Those are the freedom to express yourself, the freedom of the press to write about what they want, and forbidding the government to establish a religion."

Then you would write something like this:

> "First Amendment guarantees freedoms essential to democracy, expression, press, no established religion."

5. If your chapter is divided into sections and subsections, do this for each of them.

Only read as far as it takes to figure out what each section is about. It shouldn't take more than 10 minutes in total to quickly jot down your synopsis on the page next to that section, for all sections.

6. Once you have those jotted down, you're ready to transfer those notes of yours to a piece of paper.

Don't condense this step with the ones above. The more times you write something, the more you press that into your memory—like pressing a stamp into a piece of clay. The more times your press, the deeper the impression it makes, and the longer it stays. And keep writing by hand at this point.

Start with the notes you wrote in the table of contents. You're making an outline of what you're reading. Then transfer the notes you made in the chapter, putting your new notes right under each of your old notes so you can see the chapter headings and the annotations.

Step 2: Doing the Reading

Now that you've done that, go back and start reading the whole chapter word for word.

Think about What You're Reading

You already know what the chapter will be about; you know the main points the author will make, and how he has organized it. And you know what each section will be about. So you should be able to read without being too confused or puzzled.

Highlight Important Points

As you come to a sentence that you think is particularly important, you can highlight it or put a check mark next to it. But mostly, you should just be reading and thinking about what you've read.

Transfer Your Notes

When you finish reading the chapter, go back and transfer anything you've highlighted or checked onto your Smart Notes page. If you copy anything word-for-word from the text, be sure to put it in quote marks and write the page number next to it, because if you use it in a paper later (and these Smart Notes will come in very handy when you're writing papers), you'll have to write a citation for it, so you'll have to be able to find it again.

Take a Break!

Now put away your books and go do something else. Watch the game, fix dinner, or take the kids to a movie. Stay away for at least two hours. When you come back to studying, first read over your notes again, carefully thinking about what you're reading. You will be amazed at how much you remember.

Fast Sheets™

Fast Sheets are cards or compiled notes that you keep handy while you work on assignments.

Educators have learned how important these kinds of condensed notes are in helping students learn the material and review when it's test or paper writing time. And in eCollege, where almost all tests are open book, you can use them in your tests, too!

In the old days we called them cheat sheets, because some baddies tried to take them into class and cheat off them during tests.

In this step, you're going to take your Smart Notes and make some Fast Sheets.

Condense Your Smart Notes

Start by taking all your Smart Notes from the week. If you had a lot of reading to do, there might be a lot of notes. You need to condense them into a more manageable size, say one or two typed pages—but no more!

As you've been reading this week, attending seminars, or discussing these ideas in class, you'll find that everything has started making more sense to you. Your mind has had time to absorb the new ideas. You might have pondered them while driving to work, and maybe even had an insight or two.

Certainly, if you were asked to write any discussion questions or chat with your classmates, you would have understood even better what you were reading about. And maybe someone on a discussion thread had something intelligent to say that you hadn't thought of.

Type Up Your Fast Sheets

Now is the time to incorporate all of that into your Fast Sheets. Date a new document in MSWord, and put the subject of that week's studying at the top of the page. Then transcribe your handwritten notes onto your computer page.

As you type, make changes that are necessary; if you suddenly realize that you'd misunderstood a point, make those corrections in your notes. If you thought of something clever (or, if someone in class said something clever), type that into your Fast Sheet notes.

Save the Fast Sheets to Your Course Folder

Finally, save it all in your course folder, but also print off a page to read. For some reason, reading the piece of paper triggers a different neurological response from reading the screen. So you'll have one more round of learning, understanding, and pressing these ideas into your brain, which will further help you remember those concepts.

Show Your Professor That You Know the Material

It's not enough to learn the material—that's not going to get you an A.

Say what?

That's right, you might know the Constitution inside and out and still fail the class if you aren't able to convey that knowledge to your professor. You have to start using those new theories, concepts, and data in what you're writing on the discussion threads and in your assignments.

Use the Concepts in Your Writing

One of the ways in which you show your mastery of the material is to be able to speak and write about those ideas using the language of that discipline or profession.

In the same way, you need to master the language and terms of the subject you're studying. When you are learning about anthropology, you have to be able to discuss "artifacts" and "social systems"; when you are learning the law, you have to be able to speak of "rules" and "holdings" and "arguments."

Make a Glossary of Words and Phrases

The words and phrases that you use when writing are extremely important for showing your professor that you've learned this material. As you read and take notes, remember the words those authors used to discuss the ideas, and use the same words and phrases when *you* discuss them.

Keeping a glossary where you can write down the new words and phrases as you encounter them will be a handy tool for the times when you need to use them in your writing. You can even add a mini glossary to the bottom of every Fast Sheet for each week, so that when you're writing or answering questions, you have those terms right there to pop in. You'll be amazed at how intelligent you sound—quite instantly.

Every discipline, every profession, has its own terminology for talking about itself.

When you are learning to be a writer, you have to learn the difference between proofreading and copyediting, and you have to be able to talk about those things, using the correct words.

If my plumber said, "hand me that thingamajig that I use to unloosen these pipes." I wouldn't have much confidence in his ability to fix my plumbing.

Apply What You've Learned to Your Own Ideas

The truly brilliant student will take the ideas, theories, words, and phrases that they've been reading about and apply them to their own ideas or situations. When a professor sees this happen, he is guaranteed to be thrilled!

The way to do this is to think about how these theories or ideas might affect your life. If we didn't have the First Amendment, how would you be affected? Would you be worried about things you say on the telephone? Would you be afraid to criticize the government? When you can apply these theories to new situations, ones you haven't been reading about, you have truly learned them. Indeed, the whole purpose of paper writing is that students can apply these ideas to new situations.

The Dreaded Peer Group Assignments

Yes, we all hate them. It seems like they are designed so that slackers will get As for doing nothing, and those of us who care about our grade end up having to do all the work. But what I tell my students when they complain is, unfortunately, this is just like real life!

Why All Colleges Require Them

Sometime in the 1980s, a group of educators ran some studies and decided that the best way for students to learn was by using small groups of their peers to complete team assignments.

I know how hard it is to make this work online, because every time I go through a training program, I have to do a peer assignment, too! But if you follow these tips, you'll find that working with your team can be fun and productive.

> ### BUILDING A WORKING TEAM
>
> Your team needs to be put together like a football team; every player is assigned a different necessary task based on their personal strengths.
>
> Is someone a born organizer? Make her the team leader. Is someone an expert with grammar and spelling? He's your copy editor. Got somebody who loves researching online? Assign her the task of digging up resources.
>
> You get the picture. Use your collective talent wisely. Don't just divide the paper into five sections and assign each person a section—that's the fastest route to a D!

EIGHT STEPS FOR AN EXCELLENT
PEER GROUP ASSIGNMENT

1. Start immediately, on the very first day of the assignment so you have enough time to get it all done. Everything will take three times longer than if you did this assignment yourself. You must take that into consideration in your planning, or someone will end up desperately doing all the work during the last hour of class before it is due.

2. Assign roles for every member of the group. This is not a democracy, this is a group assignment. So you must have a group leader and assigned tasks with stated deadlines. The only voting you should do should be to elect a team leader.

3. Write a document that everyone can see (post it in your newsgroup if you can) that contains the Criteria List, the tasks for each team member, and a Task Calendar for everyone.

4. Your deadline for completing those tasks should be two days before the assignment is due.

5. Your deadline for finishing the revision of the project should be 24 hours before the project is due.

6. Your deadline for finishing the proofreading and copyediting of the project should be at least four hours before the project is due.

7. The team leader should be the one person responsible for turning in the final project.

8. Make sure everyone's name is on the project, even if someone didn't do any of the work. Remember to keep your eye on the goal: the grade that you earn. None of these classes are graded on a curve, so it doesn't affect your grade if someone gets a grade she didn't earn. And it will probably be the only good grade she makes in the class. In the meantime, you'll look good for building a team that really pulled together and got the work done. (At least, that's how your professor will see it.)

[1] You can find the *How to Study Smart Not Hard* Becky Brown study guide on the Short & Sweet Books website: www.ShortandSweetBooks.com.

7

WRITING "A" PAPERS

For most college courses, you will be assessed by the quality of papers you write for class. That's good for natural-born writers, and bad for the rest of us! Because no matter how well you know the material, if you can't write about it well, clearly, and thoroughly, you won't get an A in the course.

So knowing how to write anA paper is essential.

Kinds of Papers You Will Write

The first thing to determine when asked to write a paper is the kind of paper that's called for. Sometimes the professor will tell you: "This needs to be a persuasive paper that makes a claim and supports it with data and a strong argument."

But most often, nobody says anything about the kind of paper they want. They just tell you how many words you need and how many sources, and sometimes what your topic will be. But they say nothing about whether you'll be arguing a point, or explaining a situation, or writing an opinion.

How to Figure Out What Kind of Paper You're Supposed to Write

The truth is, there are really only three main kinds of papers you can write, and it's pretty easy to figure out which kind is called for, de-pending on the instructions you're given.

Informative Papers. If you're asked to write a paper about the Constitution and **how** it was written, you're probably going to write a "how" paper, otherwise known as an informative paper. In other words, you focus on the history and the facts. You tell the reader how it all happened, but you don't express an opinion about it.

Persuasive Papers. If you're asked to write a paper about **whether** or not you think the press has too much freedom, then you are supposed to write a persuasive paper. Persuasive papers are, essentially, argu-ments. They present one point of view, and try to convince the reader that their point of view is the right point of view. Persuasive papers depend on claims, also called opin-ions, and data to back up those claim.

Opinion Papers. Finally, if you don't have to provide any data to support your claim, then you are just writing an opinion piece (like an OpEd). That is, your prof just wants to hear what you think and why. But you don't have to provide evidence.

Informative Papers

The informative paper tells *how* to do something, how something works, or how something happened. It's all about **how**. The goal is to inform your reader, but not to argue a position or a point.

When you write an informative paper, you want to do research to provide good data about your topic. And you want to explain things thoroughly. But in the end, you're not trying to win an argument. Papers about *how* to protect children from on-line predators, *how* to winterize your car, *how* recycling can affect the weather patterns are all informative papers.

Persuasive Papers

Persuasive papers are, essentially, argu-ments. You pick a controversial topic with at least two sides, and you write an argu-ment for one of those sides. Persuasive papers use data and experts to help convince their reader that the paper's claim is right, and the opposition's claim is wrong.

Examples of persuasive paper topics are: *why* we need to take global warming seriously, *why* children shouldn't be allowed to use the Internet unsupervised, *why* the press should always be allowed complete freedom for everything they write, etc.

The persuasive paper is opinionated; however it also uses plenty of research with good data and comments from experts to prove to the reader that the stated claim is true.

Researching Your Papers

All papers for college (except fairly simple opinion pieces) require authoritative reasoning. That means you have to use *au-thorities*, experts in the field you're writing about, to provide you with the data and opinions for your papers.

Your personal opinion is required, too. But it cannot be the whole story, because just like a kid who's told that there is no Santa Clause, the reader always asks: "How do you know that? Who told you so? How can you be sure?"

Everything you write needs to be founded on good research. Your job as the scholar is to dig up those authorities, so when your professor asks, "How do you know that?" you can answer her with a list of credible sources that agree with you!

Looking Online

Where do you find these authorities? Well, in the library, of course! Just like when you were a kid. You can go to the library in your town, talk to the reference librarian, and search through stacks of books and archives of magazines and journals.

Or you can open your laptop and start your research online!

Online Libraries

These days, most schools have vast on-line libraries that you can access from the school website with your school password. This is the best place to start your research, because most of the sources for data and opinions that you find here have already been vetted and pass the approval of your school and its professors. So you can generally trust that these are credible sources.

The Internet

If you don't find what you need in the school's online libraries, you can always turn to the vast Internet. As you know, the Internet is an enormous resource of opinions and data about almost anything you can imagine. So you'll have no trouble finding something about whatever you're researching.

Please ask your professor first, to be sure that using the Internet is okay. Some teachers don't allow it.

Use Reliable Sources

But this enormity has its drawbacks. Anyone can publish a blog, or post a comment, or

What are good, reliable sources? Here's a general list:

- Sources from your school's online databases

- National publications (NYTimes, Washington Post, Newsweek, Harpers, Communication Arts)

- Journals (These are published by professional organizations, and so have editors who check facts and make sure the data is accurate.)

- Government websites (for the most part)

- National high profile non-governmental agencies (like the Red Cross, Doctors Without Borders, American Bar Association). Basically, the more high-profile, the more likely you can trust their data, since a lot of people are watching them, and pointing out errors.

- Local publications are okay too, but watch out for local biases.

even their own website. That means checking for the reliability of your sources is essential! You don't want to fill your paper with sources that turn out to be some crackpot living on the beach someplace, do you? (Trust me, you don't! Professors look at the quality of your sources, and you lose points if they are not reliable.)

That means, although you might find a white supremacist that thinks we should bring back slavery, it wouldn't be accurate to say that most Americans want a return to the antebellum days merely because you read this one source. Beware the sources you use in your paper!

Use Search Engines

How do you find these publications? Well, you use a search engine, of course! Any one of the available search engines, such as Google, Ask.com, or Yahoo is fine. They all turn up pretty much the same websites. So you can learn how to use one, and stick with it for all your searches.

The important thing to know about search engines is that they give you back lists of websites that seem to match the words you put in their search box. The closer the match, the higher up on the list that website will appear. That means the ones at the top of the list are pretty near an exact match to whatever you typed in the search box.

Try Many Different Search Words and Phrases

Do more than one search! Try many combina-

USING SEARCH TERMS

The way Google and other search engines work is they search the actual text of every website, looking for the exact combination of words you typed into the search box.

You have to be sure that you use a good combination of words and that you try many different combinations so that you can find the articles you really need.

For instance, if I want to find out about the effects of global warming on the West Coast, I could just type

"global warming"

in the search box and see what I get.

But I will get hundreds of pages, each full of lists of every website that mentions the phrase global warming somewhere in their text! Not very close to the exact topic I'm looking for.

So I'll narrow that search by typing

"global warming California"

in the box since that's exactly what I'm looking for. Now I'll only get a few dozen pages, but my list will have only websites that talk about global warming in California.

tions of words, and use several words together—never just one word. That will get you a
vast number of websites that are only
generally on topic.

Keep Searching until You Start Seeing
the Same Sources Over and Over

Try several combinations and ways of saying something in order to find all possible
articles on that subject. Each will return a
few new websites, and a few of the same
articles or websites. The ones that come up
consistently, in several different searches, are
likely to be your best sources for that topic.

Making Annotated Bibliographies

As you search for sources, you should be
keeping a bibliography. If you jot down the
reference information as you search and
read articles you won't have to try and find
these websites days later, when you'll have
to retrace your steps and try to remember where you found your information.

An annotated bibliography is a research tool made for this point in your writing process. It includes the reference for your source, with all the information you (or your reader) need to find that source again, and a short, one-paragraph summary of the article—so you remember later what that article was all about.

> SAMPLE ANNOTATED
> BIBLIOGRAPHY ENTRY:
>
> Brown, R. (2007) How To Study Smart Not Hard. Short & Sweet Books, Brooklyn, NY.
>
> This book teaches how to use study skills to speed learning and improve comprehension.

This keeps you from wasting time looking for old websites, trying to remember if this was the article that had the great quote you wanted, or if it's really about something altogether different. It saves you from rereading articles!

So, when you come to a source you think you *might* want to use in your paper, write down the author's name, the title, the publication date, that day's date, and the URL where you found it. Then read it, and write a one-paragraph synopsis of the article. Mention whatever about that particular article you think is useful.

Then go on to your next article.

When you finish writing your paper and it's time to write the dreaded reference page, you've already got it done! What? That's right, your annotated bibliography *is* your refer-ence page, once you take out the annota-tions (that one paragraph synopsis you wrote for each entry). Also, remove any articles that you didn't end up using in your paper.

This method will also ensure that you don't accidentally plagiarize any data in your pa-per—a terrible thing to happen to a good student who is trying to do the right thing.

8

Plagiarism & Copyright Infringement

One of the great benefits of the Internet is the free availability of materials and information. However, for some reason, because so much information is easy to access and read, students have begun to think that it is okay to copy and paste these writings and pictures into their papers and posts. *It is not.*

If You Think "Plagiarism Isn't That Big a Deal"

You're wrong! Plagiarism is rampant in on-line school (as well as on-ground school) probably because it's such a temptation to merely copy a beautifully written scholarly paper and paste it into your own blank document. It's exactly what your professor asked for in your assignment, and you certainly couldn't write that well, so what's the harm?

There are a number of harms, including receiving an F on the assignment, being kicked out of school, and being prosecuted for criminal copyright infringement.

Just because you **can** copy something from an Internet source and paste it into your document doesn't mean you **should**. Indeed, if you copy, you will not only be in violation of plagiarism but of federal copyright laws—a criminal offense!

If You Think "Nobody Will Ever Know if I Plagiarize"

You're wrong again! I catch students plagiarizing almost every day.

THE TRUTH ABOUT
PLAGIARISM:

If you copy someone else's words and sentences rather than writing your own words and sentences ··· You aren't learning anything

If you copy and pretend that a paper, or a paragraph, or a sentence is your own ··· You are lying

If you don't put quote marks around any sentence or collection of words that you copy from another writer (whether from a book, website, article, or even a post) ··· You are stealing

If you turn in a paper that includes large amounts of text or even ideas that are not your own, and for which you do not indicate another author ··· You are cheating

Do colleges take these kinds of infractions seriously? ... You bet they do!

Professors Can Tell

I can tell if a paper is plagiarized by the change in the student's writing, by the use of words most students don't use, by the polish of professional writing as compared to student writing.

Remember, your professors teach this stuff. They can tell when they're reading something written by a professional in the field, or another scholar or academic, or something that a copy editor has carefully worked with.

Professors Check Up on You

Whenever I read a sentence that strikes me as particularly fine, I am suspicious. I run the sentence through Google search. You would be surprised how many students don't realize that if they can run a Google search and come up with an article, I can run the same search and find the article they used!

I also use online professional tools that help teachers catch plagiarizing. Turnitin.com is a website that allows professors to upload all the student papers and run a plagiarism report; and they'll send back an email telling the professor what percentage of each paper was plagiarized. Turnitin. com even highlights the plagiarized sentences and phrases, and tells the professor where the student got those sentences.

So please do not copy any text, images, maps, sounds, or ideas from the Internet and use them in your writing or even for your personal use on your computer. It is illegal and unethical.

If You Think "Nothing Really Happens if I Plagiarize or Copy Illegally"

Wrong again! The schools I work for do take plagiarism very seriously and they require me to take it seriously, too. I have to hand out zeros for the assignment and report the student to the school administrators.

Not Knowing the Difference Won't Help

Saying "I didn't know" won't help you if you are caught plagiarizing, even if it is your first time. You're required to learn and understand the rules of plagiarism during your first class.

If you are caught plagiarizing, the least that will happen is you'll get a zero on the assignment. The worst is that this offense will go into your permanent record, you will be kicked out of school, and any other school you apply to will see that you are a plagiarizer.

Don't Take the Risk!

So if you think you can fool the system, you are playing with fire. Even if you manage to fool your professors some of the time, you won't fool them all of the time. It only takes one zero on a single assignment to drop your grade for the course below an A. The second instance of plagiarism **in your entire college career** will result in expulsion.

If You Think "All I Have to Do Is Put a Link in My Paper Somewhere"

Nope, that's not right, either! In your research and writing for school, you must clearly attribute the words and *ideas* of others when you use them in your projects and papers.

That means putting quote marks around any sentences or paragraphs in your papers that you copy from others, and providing a reference so the reader knows where those words came from. Even if you just use someone else's idea, you have to provide a citation in your paper so your reader knows that wasn't your original idea.

Plagiarism and how to quote, paraphrase, and cite your sources are a complicated system, but you'll have to learn it. Your school and many online sources have wonderful tutorials to teach you what you can and cannot do. I suggest you use them.

If you already know what to do and what not to do, here is a short list of points you can check with every paper to make sure you haven't plagiarized:

Plagiarism Checklist:

1. Did you include a reference page or Works Cited page at the end of your paper?

2. Did you put quote marks around any sentence or partial sentence that you copied exactly from your source?

3. Did you include an in-text citation immediately following that quote?

4. Did you include an in-text citation immediately following anyplace you paraphrased your source?

5. Have you made sure that not more than 10% of your paper is a direct quote?

9

MLA
& APA
STYLES

Finally, your paper is written, you've been careful not to plagiarize, you've proofread it all, and you're ready to turn it in. But wait! You have to format it according to the correct style for your department.

Say what?

I remember when I was a freshman in college getting ready to turn in my first paper, and my professor mentioned that there was a style sheet that we had to use for our papers. I couldn't understand what he was talking about. A style sheet? What was that? I'd checked the spelling, I'd put my name on it, and I'd printed it off. What more was there?

I simply couldn't get my head around this idea that different departments would have different rules about how to format a paper: rules such as those regarding the width of margins, where the title and my name go, and how to cite my sources. Not only that, they seemed to be *serious* about enforcing those rules.

Yes, they really are! In many schools, your professors simply won't accept a paper that isn't formatted correctly. And in many professions, the same is true. I knew an attorney who had his claim returned to him by the judge because the margins were not correct on his documents!

What Are Styles?

A style is the way a publisher or an institution requires that your paper be formatted. It includes what sort of information you must have in your references, whether you must have a title page, and whether to use footnotes or endnotes.

Really, anything having to do with the choices you make about how your paper looks is in these style sheet rules. And you thought those decisions were up to you!

The Two Primary College Styles

There are two main styles that you are likely to encounter in your online school (although you should be aware that there are at least seven other styles that are used in this country). Those two main styles are MLA and APA. Most English departments use MLA. Most social science and business departments use APA.

I am not going to go over the particulars here, because they are very detailed and often slightly different at each college. (Sigh . . . yes, I know. Could they make this any harder on the students?)

Ask Your Professor for the Style

What you have to do is ask your professor for the style sheet, or the manual that her department recommends. Then when you're ready to turn in your paper, go through that sheet point by point and make sure you are following the style exactly!

That's the way we all do it, even the professionals. So no moaning and groaning— this is just a fact of life.

Available Online Resources

Oh, but wait! I almost forgot. There's an online tool that will help you. That's right, there is an online tool called the Citation Machine. It won't format your entire paper, but it will format those citations and references that are so irritatingly difficult to do right.

Go to www.citationmachine.net.

On the left-hand side of your screen, you will see a menu for MLA, APA, and Chicago. Choose the style that you're required to use, and then fill in the boxes with the data that's asked for and click the button. The Citation Machine will spit out a perfect in-text citation and reference for your paper. You can just copy and paste it.

So that speeds up *that* process!!

There are all kinds of other online resources that will help you with everything about writing a paper, including style sheets, citations, grammar, and punctuation. For a list, please see the appendix in this book.

In Closing . . .

I hope that now you have a much better understanding of how college works, in general, and how Internet colleges work, in particular. Knowledge is power, and I expect you

to put this new power to use immediately
to improve your grades in all your classes.

Return to this book as you need it; if you run
into problems with an instructor, it would be
helpful to review how professors evaluate
their students and what your best methods
for dealing with your professor might be.

Don't think like a student—think like an adult!
Think about your goal, earning that degree
and getting the best grades while you do it,
and then decide on your course of action.

When writing papers or studying textbooks,
you might want to refresh your memory
about the Fast Sheets and Smart Notes. You'll
have to practice these a few times before
they come easily and naturally to you.

Finally, don't forget that college is about learning and improving. So take every criticism and
every comment from a professor or a classmate as a valuable insight into how you might
improve. That's what the A students are doing.

And now that you're one of that crowd,
I know you'll be doing it, too.

Good studying!

Appendixes

Appendix A: Glossary of Terms

Accelerated classes – An entire semester's worth of assignments crammed into 5-10 short weeks.

Annotated bibliography – A research tool made for this point in your writing process. It includes the reference for your source, with all the information you (or your reader) need to find that source again, and a short, one-paragraph summary of the article—so you remember later what that one was all about.

APA style – A particular way of formatting your paper before you turn it in. There are two main styles that you are likely to encounter in your online school (although you should be aware that there are at least seven other styles used in this country). They are MLA and APA. Most English departments use MLA. Most social science and business departments use APA.

Assignment calendar – A calendar that you create by noting when each assignment is due, and when you need to complete each *part* of that assignment. Having this will make sure you stay on schedule for everything you have to turn in.

Asynchronous – Courses that never require you to be online at the same time as anyone else in

145

your class, including your instructor. The beauty of asynchronous courses is that you really can do that work any time that you can fit it in. Even if that is in the middle of the night.

Attaching documents

- When you turn in a paper or other document to your professor for grading, you will have to attach that paper to your post to send it. Attaching just means that when you send the post to the school's server, a copy of the paper goes along with it.

Most software programs allow you to attach a document by clicking on a button that says "Attach" or on a little paperclip icon. Once you click on that button, a window opens up, allowing you to type in the name of the document or find it on your computer.

Bulletin board – A board usually made of cork that you stick notes to with a pin. Also, a space on the school's computer where you post messages to your professors and classmates. Classes are conducted on newsgroups, which are also called message boards or bulletin boards. Newsgroups work very much like real bulletin boards. People post notes on the bulletin board and other people read those notes and post replies.

Copyright – A legal right everyone has as soon as they create something. If you copy what someone else has created, you have infringed their copyright—a criminal offense!

Course load – How many classes you are allowed (or required) to take at once. For online schools, this is usually not more than two.

Discussion questions (DQs) – Questions about the materials that your professor posts for you and your classmates to discuss. Talking about these ideas helps you learn and understand them better.

Distance education – Also known as online universities and eCollege, this is a method of delivering college-level programs and courses to students who cannot sit in the same physical classroom as their instructors.

eCollege - Going to college online. Also, a web-based platform that some online universities use to deliver their class materials.

eMail - Messages that you send from your computer over the Internet.

Excel – A software program from Microsoft Office Suite that allows you to make spreadsheets on your computer.

Fast Sheets – Becky Brown's system for compiling your notes into handy cards that you can easily use when you study or write papers.

Grade Point Average (GPA) – The grade you are earning. GPA is calculated by adding all the grades you've earned in each class and dividing the sum by the total of classes you've taken. Also, you can figure out your GPA (and so, your grade) in any class by adding all the points you've earned so far and dividing that sum by the number of points *it is possible* to earn so far.

Grievance - The official record you file (or is filed against you) for wrong behavior in the classroom. Your professor can file a grievance against you for misbehaving, and you can file a grievance against your professor for giving you an unfair grade.

Helpdesk – The place you call whenever you have problems with the software or hardware, including not being able to access your class, forgetting your password, changing your login name, etc.

Individual newsgroup (ING) - A bulletin board that only you and your professor can see.

Informative paper - A paper that merely presents the facts and not an opinion.

Internet technology (IT) - Everything having to do with software, hardware, and the Internet. The IT people man the helpdesk, and help you when you have problems with these things.

Late policy - The policy your professor enforces

about when you can turn in late assignments, and how many points you lose if they're late.

Message board (MB)
– Classes are conducted on newsgroups, which are also called message boards or bulletin boards. Newsgroups work very much like real bulletin boards. People post notes on the bulletin board and other people read those notes and post replies.

Microsoft Word (MSWord)
– The standard word processing program required in every online university. It is not the same thing as Microsoft Works, WordPerfect, or Notepad.

MLA style – A particular way of formatting your

paper before you turn it in. There are two main styles that you are likely to encounter in your online school (although you should be aware that there are at least seven other styles used in this country). They are MLA and APA. Most English departments use MLA. Most social science and business departments use APA.

Newsgroups (NG) -
Classes are conducted on newsgroups, which are also called message boards or bulletin boards. Newsgroups work very much like real bulletin boards. People post notes on the bulletin board and other people read those notes and post replies.

149

On-ground school – Traditional classes that are held in a brick and mortar classroom, with a professor standing in front of you.

Online school – Classes that are held on a website or using other Internet software. Your professor and your classmates are all in different locations and often never even meet in real time.

Outlook Express (OE) – Software from the Microsoft Office Suite that collects and sends email, and lets you access your newsgroups. Some schools use OE to conduct their online classes.

Paper criteria list - A list you write of all the requirements you have to be sure your paper meets.

Persuasive paper - A paper that makes a claim and supports that claim with data. An argument.

Plagiarism - Taking the words or ideas of another author and passing them off as your own. Forgetting to put quote marks around a quote, and forgetting to provide the citation and reference are considered plagiarism.

Posting - Posting is how you get messages that you write on your computer up to the school's computer. When you put a message on a bulletin board or newsgroup, it's called "posting" the message.

Appendix B: Online Resources

You are among the first generation of college students to have the vast resources of the Internet available to you for all sorts of research. So learn to turn there first when you are confused.

Below are a list of some of my favorite writing, studying, and grammar websites. Sometimes you need a tutorial to help you understand, and sometimes just reading about it in different words will make the light-bulb go on. So give these websites a shot.

How to Write a Five-Paragraph Paper

These websites include great discussions and tutorials about how to write a five-paragraph paper—the building block of all papers.

http://www.gc.maricopa.edu/English/writing.html

http://www.geocities.com/jk102.geo

http://essayinfo.com/essays/5-paragraph_essay.php

http://www.englishdiscourse.org/

5.paragraph.essay.format.htm

How to Write Thesis Statements

These are great places to get help
with your thesis statement.

http://www.wisc.edu/writing/Handbook/

Thesis.html

http://www.rpi.edu/web/writingcenter/

thesis.html

http://www.indiana.edu/~wts/

pamphlets/thesis_statement.shtml

http://leo.stcloudstate.edu/acadwrite/

thesistatement.html

http://www.unc.edu/depts/wcweb/

handouts/thesis

Help with APA Style

Citation Machine

http://www.citationmachine.net
If you gather the data, this online tool will format the citations and references for you!

APA Style

http://www.apastyle.org/
The official website of APA Style

The OWL at Purdue

http://owl.english.purdue.edu/owl/resource/560/01/

Help with MLA Style

Citation Machine

http://www.citationmachine.net
This works for MLA style, too!

The Owl at Purdue

http://owl.english.purdue.edu/owl/resource/ 557/01/MSWord Tutorials

MSWord Help

If you need help learning to use your MSWord program, there are a number of free, online tutorials for you to use. Here are a few I like:

http://www.bcschools.net/staff/WordHelp.htm
http://office.microsoft.com/en-us/ training/CR061832731033.aspx
http://www.internet4classrooms. com/on-line_word.htm
http://www.learnthat.com/ courses/computer/word/
http://netforbeginners.about.com/ od/learnmsword/Learn_Microsoft_ Word_97_2000_2002_2003.htm

PowerPoint Help

These PowerPoint tutorials can help you improve your skills from the sim-

pelest presentations to the most complex. They can be found at:

http://office.microsoft.com/en-us/train-
ing/CR061832731033.aspx http://www.
bcschools.net/staff/PowerPointHelp.htm

Excel Help

But for you more math-inclined students,
you'll find Excel is your best friend. Use it
wisely—learn the program! Here are tutorials that I hear are quite good:

http://www.usd.edu/trio/tut/excel/
http://www.fgcu.edu/sup-
port/office2000/excel/
http://www.bcschools.net/staff/ExcelHelp.htm

Where to Get Instant Messaging Software

You just have to know their IM name.
(Mine is ProfBecky. You can IM me, too!)

http://www.aim.com/index.adp

About the Author

Rebecca Brown, M.A., has taught more than 3000 courses online. She teaches English, humanities, and critical thinking courses. Becky also tutors students in study skills and paper writing.

Becky is the author of several Short & Sweet Books titles, including *HOW TO STUDY SMART NOT HARD* and *HOW TO MAKE As in eCOLLEGE*, which can be found at http://www.ShortandSweetBooks.com.

She loves to talk to students about their on-line school experiences and is always happy to answer questions, help with problems, and applaud successes in the eCollege world.

If you would like to be tutored by Becky, or take one of her study skills seminars, please email her at:

BeckyBrown@ShortandSweetBooks.com

www.ingramcontent.com/pod-product-compliance
Lightning Source LLC
Chambersburg PA
CBHW032001040426
42448CB00006B/446